In loving memory of William.C.Kirk and Dr Elee Kirk

Poems from the life of Willie Kirk, his experiences of how he saw the world in the late 1960s and early 1970s. From his love of hiking and athletics to the nature that surrounded him. Tragically Willie drowned at the age of 36 doing what he loved, surrounded by nature, punting on the Thames in Oxford.

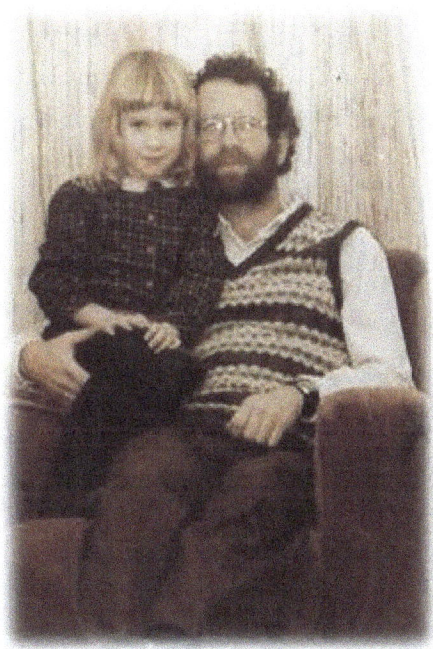

Some of the photographic illustrations were taken by Willie's daughter Dr Elee Kirk. She also loved nature, the touch of grass and the swirling clouds. Heartbreakingly, Elee also passed away at the age of 38 from cancer.

Amy Oliver is the daughter and sister of the aforementioned (who also contributed to the photography). She has found great inspiration in her family members and wanted to keep their memories alive.

Contents

Hiker

The rain is cold upon the mountains.

Out there the wind is driving

Hard grey mist down from the sky

Across my view.

I stand here

Beneath the dampened sweetness of the trees,

Man planted conifers,

Huddled within my anorak, but dry

To a degree,

Breathe it all in,

Wipe a strand of sodden rain conducting hair

From just above my eyes.

Now I debate.

Shall I wait here, just above the hill line,

For the shower to abate,

Continuing my walk across the open hillside,

Through the long grass and heather,

Damp around my feet;

Or shall I climb up through the forest,

Trackless dark but dry,

Until, emerging from its blanket, darker green,

Upon the higher side,

I find myself in striking distance of the peak.

Ponder a while.

You know that life in its simplicity

Is good.

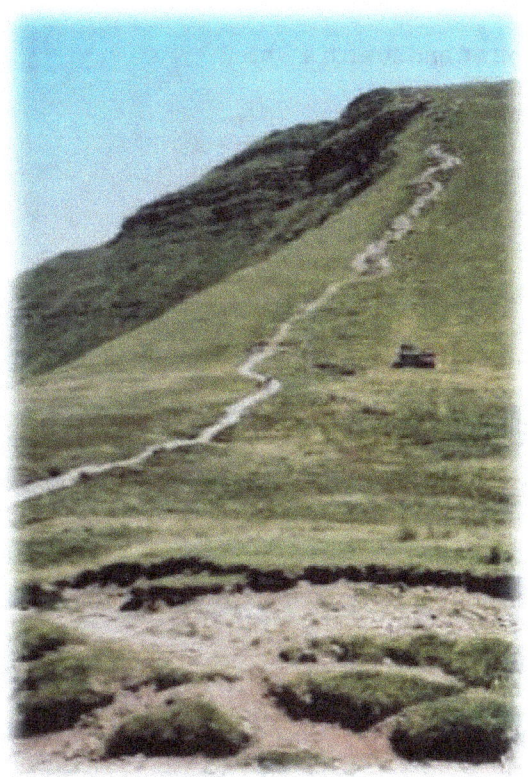

The Passing of the Giants

"The giants are dormant now.

Hush child, do you not know that they are sleeping;

And though at interval, one

Prodded into action,

May yawn and stretch a while,

Yet they will sleep now,

Such as do remain."

"Oh father you saw them, you saw them run,

Fleet footed and powerful, you saw the strength,

Stirring the blood of a small dreaming boy.

Where are the giants gone? Why do they sleep?"

"When they were dreaming hard,

Not tiring, never tiring child,

But merely using their full strength,

Then there was power child, such you have never seen,

Brute power in the quivering muscles, body strength

Of steel.

But child

The gentle giants are dormant now,

And there is sadness in my heart

That you have never seen the power,

Have never thrilled before the sight of one such giant

In his headlong flight.

That you have never felt emotions that I lost

So many years ago."

Love Ever Lost

There are many aspects of my life which do not change.

In spring the grass shoots green,

And quickly spreads to cover all the world beneath its dew damp emerald cloak.

In summer there is a promise of sun

Which never comes.

Sometimes the sky is blue in other quarters of the dome,

But ever yet the clouds conspire between the source of light and me.

And then in autumn all the fruit is small and hard,

Bitter to eat, or blighted by some worm.

And so the winter comes,

With rain on rain, the earth is mud beneath my feet,

And never the purity of Northern snow

To blot the aftermath from view.

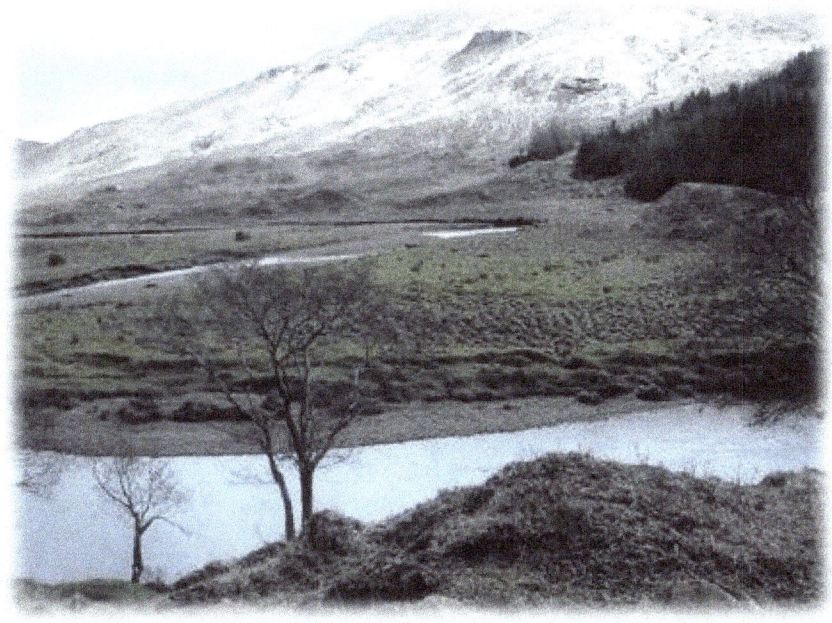

In the Beginning

Existence is. Time starts

His long relentless march,

Already doomed to motion through eternity;

And in his new born infancy his howls

Seep through to consciousness, awakening it,

And thrust it deep into the awareness of itself.

Existence fights. The womb is dark and warm;

A blind deaf feeling of its being comfort gives

To the yet untutored Entity which is.

Then revelation comes, It sees

The long inevitable journey

Which must be trod, and, ageing, forces time

Into a motion suited to its plan.

It concentrates its power, intent upon a single fact,

Which must be if the plan may run its course.

The power of thought is focused, and command

Rings through the empty corridors of space,

Till time has learned the course that he must take,

His way lit by the Being's new found power,

The fundamental cry, "Let there be light!"

Daybreak

The dawn is here.

A chill upon the air now holds,

A dewy mist evaporates to day.

I saw, but one song of a lonely herald since,

The first pink tinge upon the eastern sky.

And as it grows,

Acquiring all of majesty and power,

A glorious magic spreads across the heaven.

A cloud,

A single puff of lamb fleece on the sky,

Takes fire,

The conflagration spreading

Turns each one

Into a herald for the King of day,

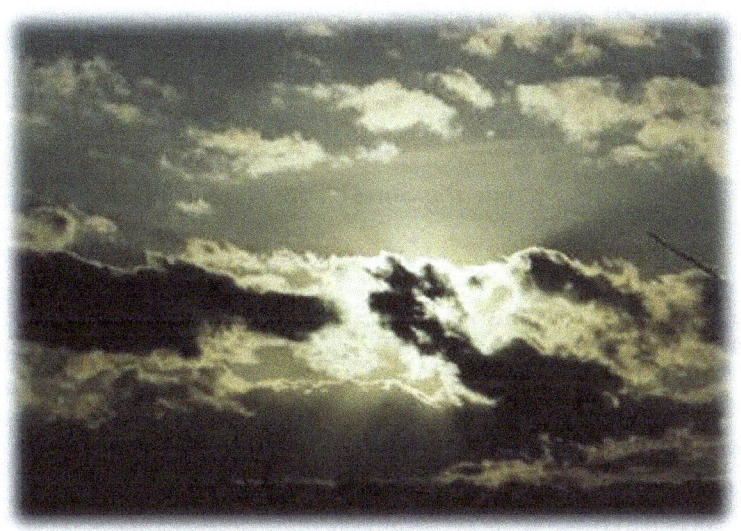

Rising in lonely splendour from his sleep.

The pink now shifts

With swift but subtle change

To orange, palest green,

And golden glory flaming 'cross the sky.

Then over the horizon shows a drop of liquid gold,

Grows,

Slow quick changing to a diamond fire,

Unviewable intensity

Of life now flooding on the slowly walking world.

And so I stand

And watch the oft repeated birth of day,

The miracle of life upon our earth.

And this is mine

And made for none but me

Alone.

Sanpshot II

So comes the sunset.

Standing by the sea

I watch the flame die.

See the burning gold sink slowly

Down into the depths of murmuring sound.

The quietly deep resounding waves,

Breaking their hearts across the level sand

A million miles away.

Reflect the shattered image

Of the slowly dimming,

Quickly dying

Beauty in the sky.

Then for a time the world stands still,

And during all this time,

This short eternity,

The earth and I may take communion,

Make love,

And life is very good.

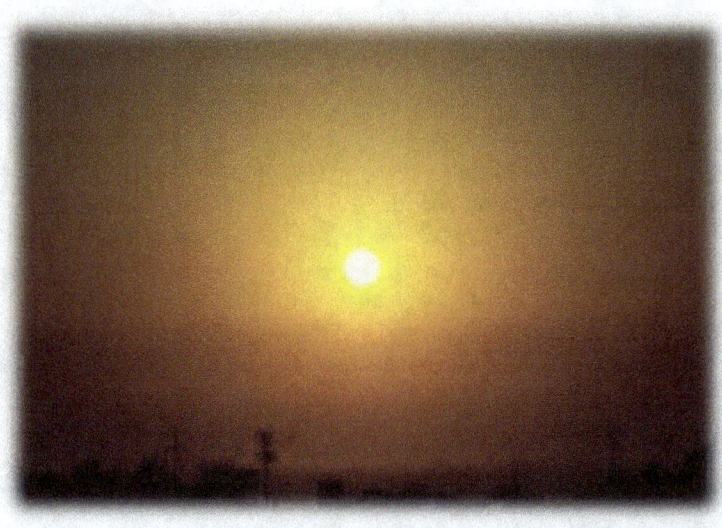

Athlete

The night is warm,

So I put on my running shoes

And head out for the road.

The stars are bright,

And it is pleasant, floating lightly through the shadow of the moon.

In even time the shoes go lightly on their way,

And I, immersed within my body,

Dream of mighty deeds,

The victors I will vanquish in my time.

The miles go by.

I put my hands upon my thighs

And feel the muscles slap like rubber

Up against the bone.

It sees too much,

There is not strength within

To take more than a few unsteady steps.

And yet

A thousand times a mile—

How many miles have gone beneath my feet tonight?

And so,

Breathing in rhythm with the steps I take,

I travel on.

The light clad, lighter stepping runner

In the night.

Day's End, Oslo, 1968

And then there were the evenings.

All afternoon we'd walk,

Or sit in contemplation

Underneath the tall pines

That surrounded some small lake

High in the hills.

Then, as the sun sank, we'd go higher,

And see it slowly sink into the sea

Beyond the glittering gold and shining silver of the fjord.

Black silhouettes of islands

Seen dimly through the sunset tinted air.

And I have no experience to match these Northern sunsets.

Never before or since has all the air

Turned red before the darkness,

Never such jewels as the flashing

Blazing beauty of the fjord.

Never such solitude,

So many poems

Unwritten and unread.

Departure

And now

The hour draws near.

I look around at those who must remain

And think that this is hardship and no gain,

While I can see the things they do not know

And I must go.

And you,

From you I hear,

"You must be mad, to not desire to leave,

For we would willing part and never grieve."

But I, who will walk out, as you say, free,

I cannot see.

Although

My sight is clear

And I can see adventure in my life,

I also see the times of sadness, strife.

Behind me leave security and peace,

Which now must cease.

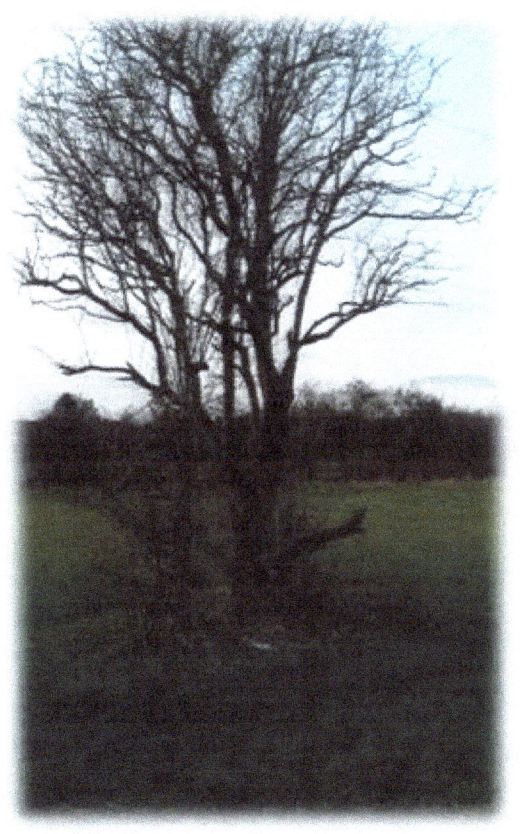

And yet

When gone a year

Or two, I know this place will fade from mind,

For loves are lost, affections left behind.

And I will live a life away from those

With whom I rose.

So I

Will go, through dear

May be the penalty of broken ties;

They may be yet reborn in other guise,

And new and better yet could still be seen

Than what has been.

And so I will not fear

To go out happy to a clear new light,

To leave my doubts behind, put out of sight

Like twilight clouds, and as in faith I grow,

Rejoicing go.

Oxford Summer

The lazy afternoon drifts slowly by,

Swirls gently round us.

And we ourselves drift slowly,

Onward,

Up the river.

The streaks of sun

Between the branches of the overhanging
trees

Are dancing on the surface of the water,

And across your face,

Across your lazy, sleepy eyelids.

The punt drifts slowly up the river

As all the world lies in contented peace,

And life is very good.

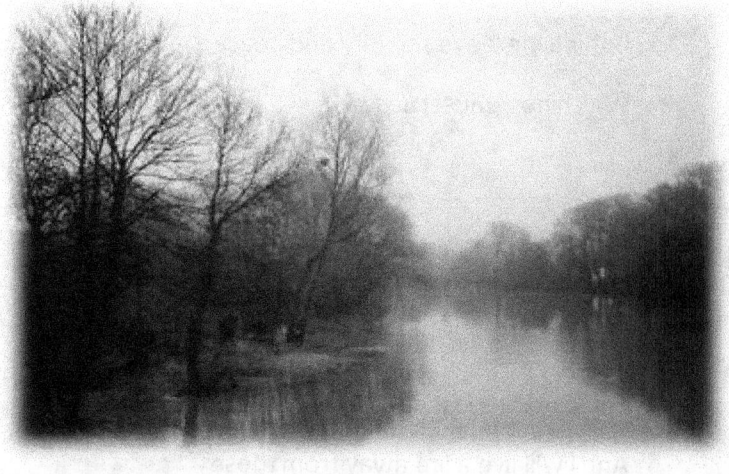

I, Adam

The place had had no name

Before his coming.

Just a green and pleasant valley,

Somewhere on the surface of the earth.

He wandered through the trees

Beside the river.

Ate the many fruits and berries

That hung in the luscious clusters from the trees.

It was a peaceful world,

And thus he named it,

Gave it a name of peace and love,

Calling the lovely valley Eden.

And thus his time was passed

Through all that season,

Ordering life and giving names,

Living the life of peace in Eden.

And through the hazy heat,

After the moontime,

He would sleep beneath a cypress,

Content because he knew not discontent.

So as he deeply slept

Beneath the cypress,

One hazy heated afternoon,

The presence was, and he woke to find Eve.

And Eve was honey sweet,

Her perfect features,

Skin made like the skin of peaches,

Full of youth, mature and womanhood.

And then divided flesh,

Again, united,

Became as one and this was love,

The first love, pure and undefiled.

Why can we not return

Once more to Eden?

How did we lose our innocence?

Why are we punished for our father's sins?

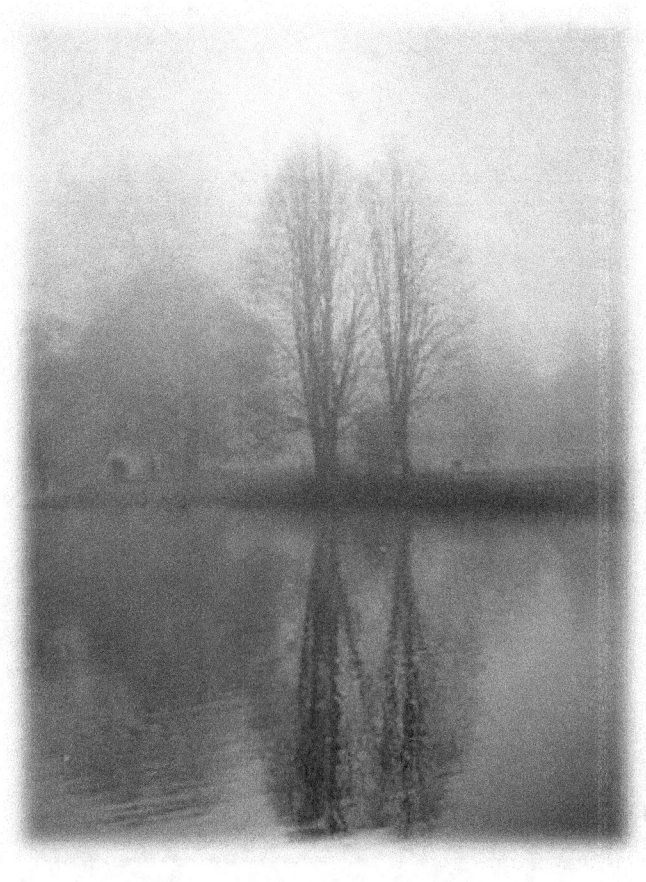

Moth

I sit before the window,

Looking out into impenetrable dark,

See only my own glass-distorted image

That returns my stare.

Tap tap.

The sound is loud and sharp.

I look towards it, see the shadow

Ghostly grey, that fires in from the gloom

To dash itself against

The unseen force that keeps it from the light.

Why does it not get broken?

Those cobweb wings should break

So hard their owner dashes them against

The flat unyielding panes.

The sound is sharp and clear

Tap. Tap.

The moth against the window pane.

I flick the switch

And listen to the silence

Of my now departed friend.

Photograph from a Sunday Supplement

Their God had made them,

They were very beautiful.

Their velvet skins touched close

As they stood cheek by cheek

Together.

The photograph was taken,

We were told,

Somewhere upon the streets of Harlem,

City of the dead.

And they were very beautiful,

Both he and she,

The cousins,

Wishing to escape

And live.

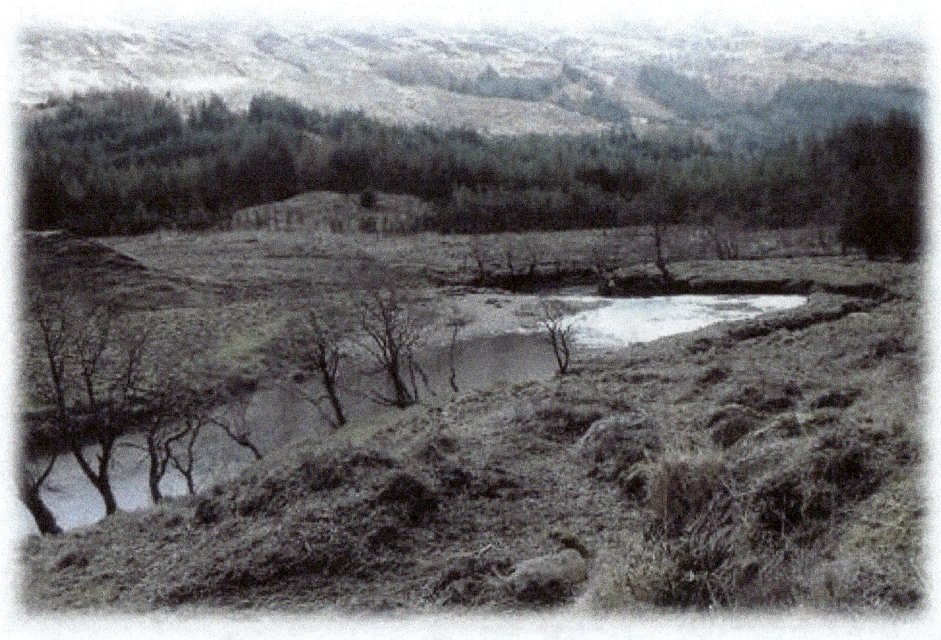

Prelude

So come away with me and I

Will show you many wonders strange,

Things your mind may never yet have known.

Things you cannot comprehend

Till I have shown the reason why,

When we unto Elysia have flown.

And I will show where mighty centaurs

Graze upon Olympian heights;

And you may ride one if it so shall please.

You will see where gods disport them

Down by silver lakes and streams,

And dance between Ambrosia bearing trees.

I will show a crystal fountain,

Thundering high beyond the clouds;

So high the diamond waters ne'er touch ground.

And let you hear a magic river

From the ends of universe,

From which Apollo all his music found.

So come away with me and see

A garden made for pure delight,

Of flowers of dawn a garland I will weave.

And there amid the hyacinths

Will place it round your tender throat,

And teach you how to love and never grieve.

For we shall walk Olympus' mount

Where softest grass is emerald green

And there are things no mortal man has seen.

For I, the mighty son of Saturn,

Wish to feast me on your beauty,

Till you have for a time a goddess been.

The First Athletes

We came over the rise running fleet as the wind,

Sensation of travelling free,

As we flowed through the grass never touching the ground,

Hard breathing in rhythm the only heard sound

From my two companions and me.

For our bodies are hardened and tuned to the work;

All the muscles and tendons are strong,

We are fleetest of foot, we are strongest of arm,

And the punishment renders our bodies no harm,

Though the chase or the combat be long.

For we call ourselves hunters, the men of the tribe,

And we carry our spears as we run,

And our quarry is tiring, we tell from his trail,

So we run ever faster, up hill and down dale,

And on 'til the chase be done.

Solitude

I must return to the high hills,

To be alone

And not feel I am lonely.

I must return to the high hills.

I must return to the old moors,

To the lost tracks

High above the world of men.

I must return to the old moors.

I must return to the to the white skies.

No sun, no cloud,

No rain, only the clean wind.

I must return to the white skies.

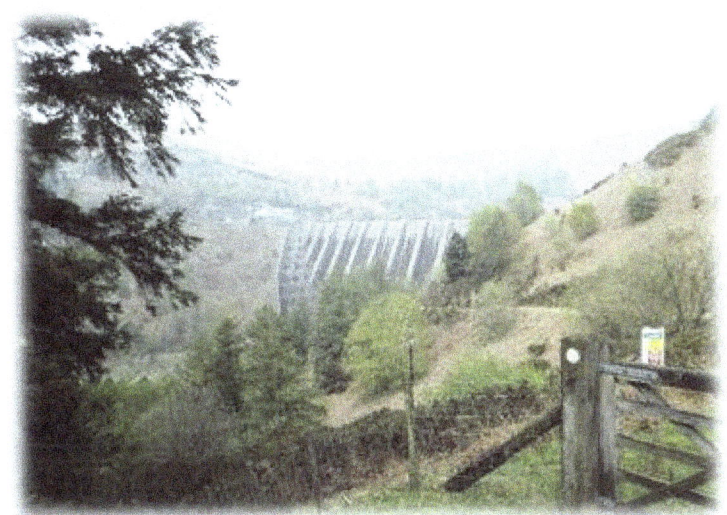

I must return to the high hills,

To the hard land,

Where my soul is purified.

I must return to the high hills.

The Children of the Great God Pan

There was no one else around.

In dual solitude we walked that sunny afternoon

Down through the woods.

The grass beneath our unshod feet

Was soft and springy, cool and fine and green.

Above the sun was hot

But we in shade were walking

Underneath the shelter of the trees,

Marvelling at the silence filled by birdsong

Then came the other silence.

Hush. the birds are stilled,

The sounds of ocean from the leaves above our heads

Just........ceased.

Then soft, far from the distance,

Came the music.

Music of recorder? Pipes?

Yes music shrill with purity,

The music of the pipes

Came from the far away

Mysterious, sun dappled, lost heart of the woods.

We knew the tune, the rhythms of the ancient people

Stirred within our veins,

And for the moment

We and all that lived about us,

Shivered in the air

Filled with presentiment

And refound knowledge of our people's long forgotten youth.

The Lament

It was good that we should have stood together,

You and I friend,

Side by side,

On the day of the long battle

Beneath the high shoulder of the black mountain

Fought beneath the clouds

And mists of the black mountain;

That we fought all that day

Against the raiders from the sea

With the black shields.

Fought for freedom.

That we fought for freedom side by side.

All this was good,

And now, with you, is past.

And so, tonight,

The pipe play lonely

On the battleground of ancient time,

Where men were men

And you the truest of them all.

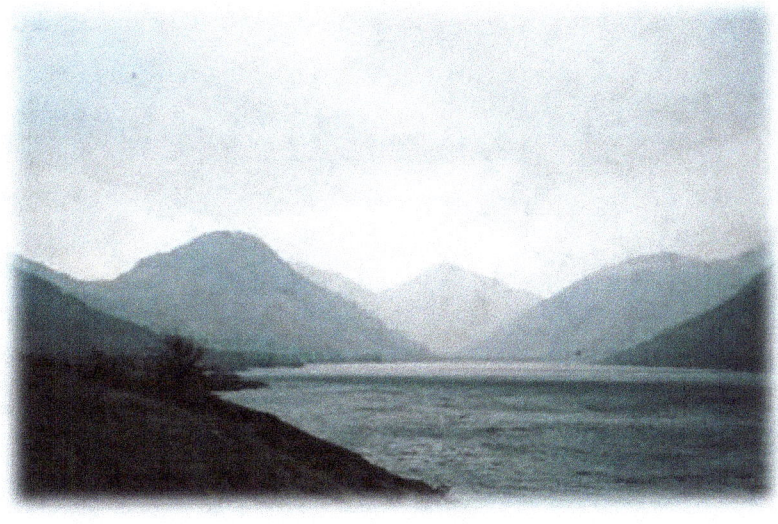

The Dreamer

Today I have been dreaming.

Dreaming dreams of many places, strange times and forgotten people.

Dreaming of swords and kisses, death and immortality,

Of love and non-existence, of myself.

My dreams drift slowly through the hazy, lazy, heated misty sea that is my mind.

Dreams in misty colours,

Dreams to remove me from this harsh world of reality,

Transport me to the furthest part of time,

Beyond the end of this or any other universe.

I can be happy in the unreality of dreams,

They cannot hurt me.

I will dream forever if I may.

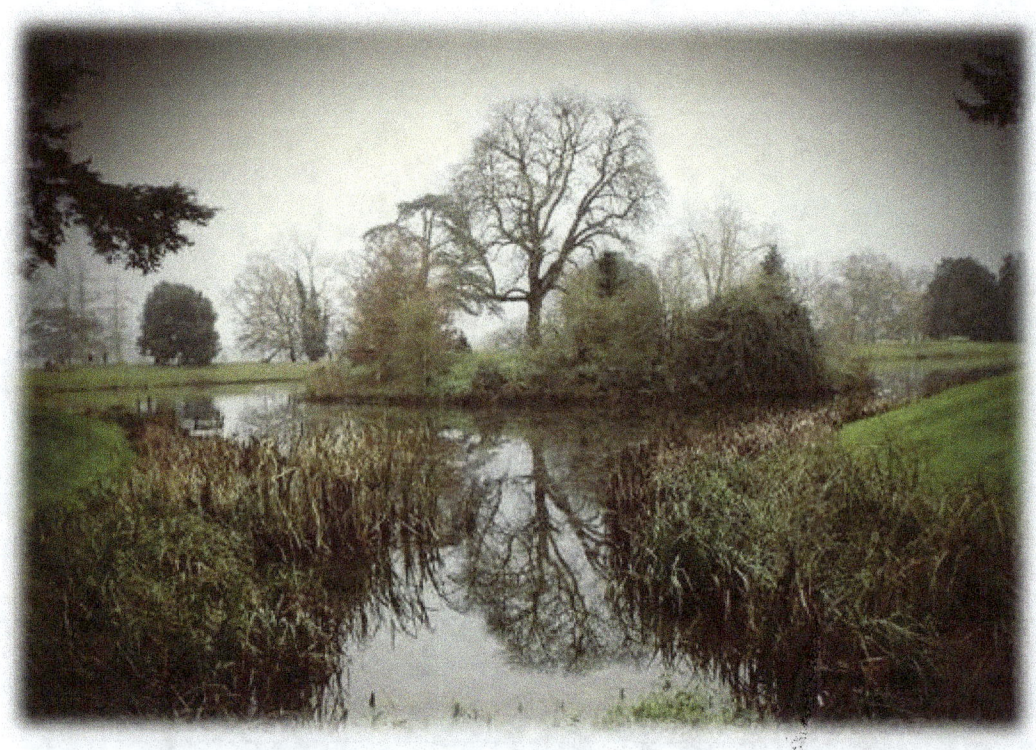

The Moment

A magic moment

Captured for eternity

Within my mind.

The silence reinforced

By far-away songs of the blackbirds

Deep within the woods,

Stretching to infinity on either side.

And so we drifted silent

Down the windless surface of the river.

And in that moment's stillness

Turned minds inward,

Finding thus

The fullness of the beauty

Of this peaceful

Moment,

Trapped for ever in eternity.

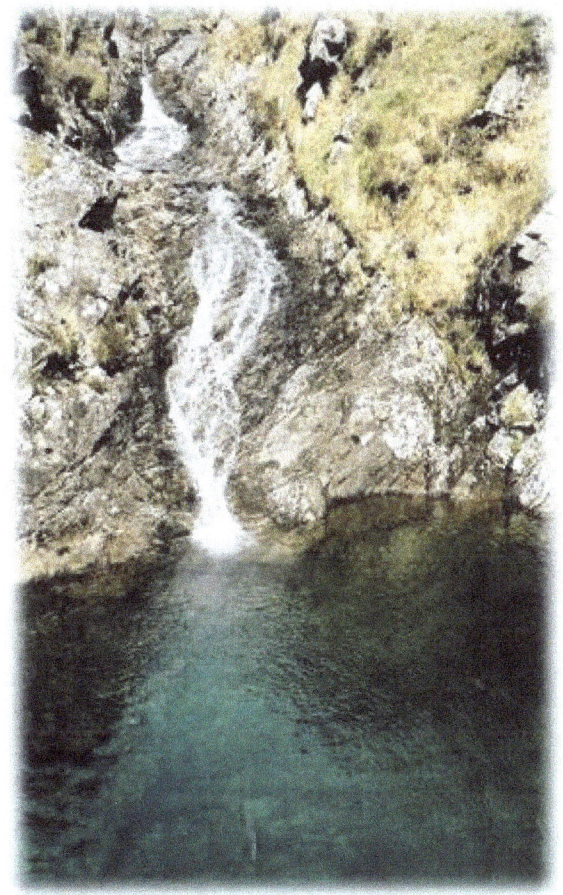

The Second Dream

The fire is cold, the flame has died;

The grey rocks all the eye can see.

The land is old,

And old to all eternity.

We landed on a long dead world,

No life on barren rock we saw.

The land is old

And inhospitable and raw.

On the mountain I stand now

And set the thoughts I'm thinking down.

The land is old,

And under an ancient dusty gown.

I cannot tell, I cannot see

The wastes of eternity.

The land is old,

And old as long as time shall be.

The Silences

First there was peace.

Then man, destroyer came.

Dawn.

Then, when at his brother's hand the first man died,

There was that shock of silence.

Later.

Then when night stilled the clash of swords

There was that shock of silence.

Not long since.

Then when the guns stopped

There was that shock of silence.

Maybe.

Then when the bombs, the race, the fight,

The loving, hating, killing, being born,

The living and the dying,

The world, the sun, the universe

And time

All stopped together.

The only thing was the appalling shock of silence.

The Visionary

"One day you will be taken up

In the arms of a tall fair stranger,

Who shall sail in from the East."

"Is this the truth?

Oh promise me that it is true,"

"I cannot promise child.

It may not be.

My words are words used by the dumb,

Who cannot speak.

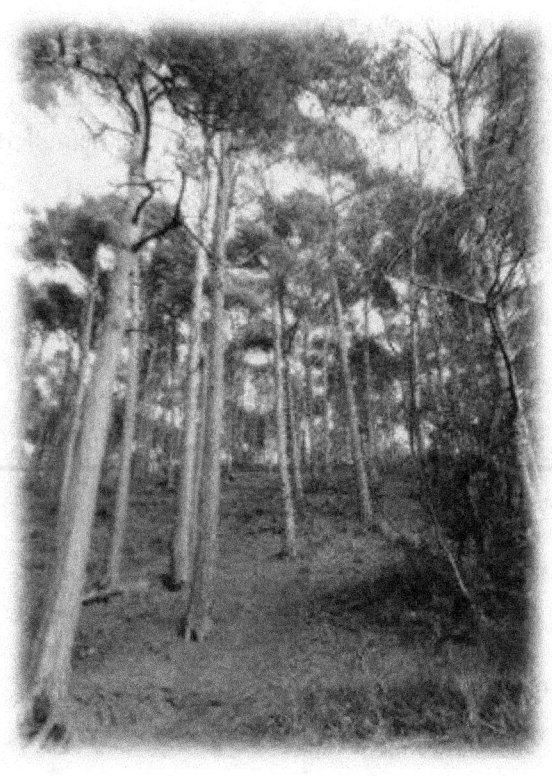

My visions are those of the blinded man,

Obscured by mists of sorrow.

And the sounds I hear are those

Heard by a man who has

Benn deafened by the war.

It may not be.

The sunshine may not last beyond this hour.

She looked,

And saw there was no wind or cloud upon the sky.

Where are my people?

I sing for the lost virtues of the other men,

The men of time gone by;

For truth and honour

And the bonds of kinship

With the men who bear my name.

But the days are gone and lost

When bearded warriors

Chiefs and leaders of their kinsmen,

Knew to be men,

And carried with their pride

The shield of leather

And the two edged sword of manhood.

Afterwards

Tonight I stood out in the rain,

Composed a poem of unutterable sadness.

My own obituary closely intertwined

About a love song written just for you.

And So We Too Once More Shall Be Good Friends.

(Paradise Lost 1968)

For me, you were like some drug,

Which, drowning all the poignancy of real emotion

By its mind enveloping effect,

Permitted me to wander far

Among the dreams is gave me.

And now, as is so usual in each such case,

The symptoms of withdrawal come.

The mind distressed,

Emotional confusion, hope, despair, relief

And hopelessness,

And tears that creep upon me unobserved,

Are all the world I know.

But still I know,

I've been through all this somewhere once before;

I can survive,

And even wonder, in a moment of lucidity,

About the next time.

Love Song

Sing, my love,

And in the dark waters of you eyes the sunrise sings.

Somewhere beyond your gentle smile

The lands of happiness are waiting

And the sky is warm.

I am the world.

Above you and around you

I am the strong one, gentle in your dreams;

And in my velvet depths

I would envelope and enfold

The one I love.

Regret

I am a butterfly.

You and I may not make love

Because you are

A caterpillar.

The Fifth Love Thoughts

I dream of desire

And I desire dreams.

I speak unto my friends in images not words

And the moon of my desire has yet to rise.

The Sixth Love Thoughts

Today I saw her smile.

She smiled at me.

And so I thought to linger for a while,

But she has gone.

The moment quickly passed,

The memory lingers on.

If she could be with me,

Could be around,

On hand, to see the things that she should see,

That would be good.

But it may never happen

That is understood.

The tree is just in flower,

The fruit unripe,

Not to be picked until the proper hour.

Then at that time

The sweetness the I taste

Will be forever mine.

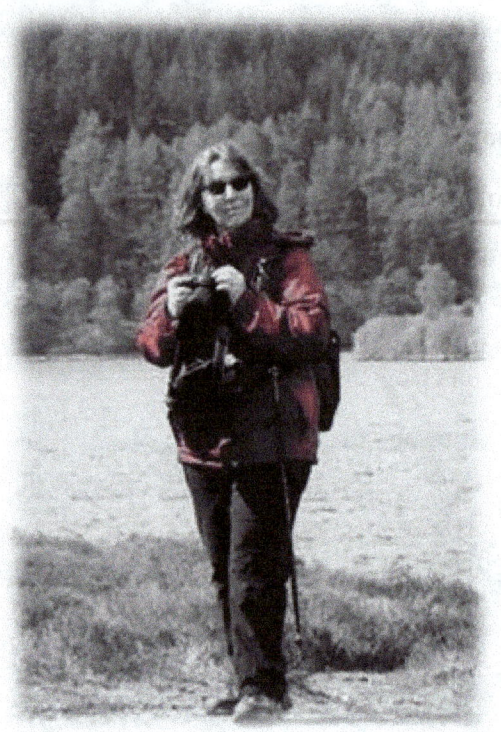

The Seventh Love Thoughts

Sunshine and shadow,

Brightness and darkness,

Both are traced across my mind;

In clear sharp bars,

Or in a rippling, dancing pattern,

Such as trees in windy winter cast upon the ground.

And which are you?

I know not.

Whether you are the sun

That glitters through the bars,

Or are you the shadow, even now depriving me

Of sunlight that I crave,

Or you are both or neither,

These are things which I cannot yet see;

And will not

Till the sun's strong heat

Consumes the bars with fire,

Or till the shutters slam upon my sun

For evermore.

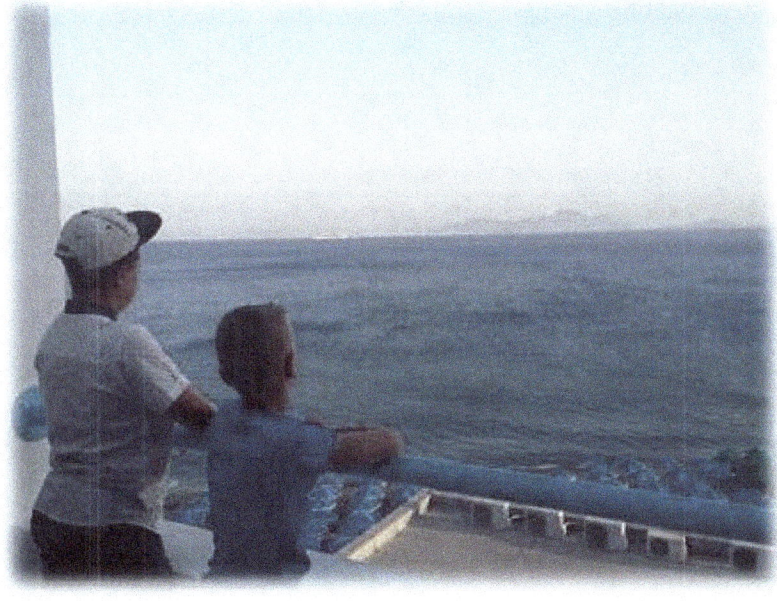

Lindy: The First Poem

Lindy, I have been taken by surprise,

For it is not so long ago I did not know you.

It was so strange, for all I did was look into your eyes.

Lindy, I did not know that kisses tasted sweet.

How freely was this sweetness given by you.

Last night you gave with joy and made my happiness complete.

Lindy, though total of our hours together won't be long,

Your love has given me lifetime memories of you.

For Lindy comes to me and she inspires a lover's song.

Lindy: The Third Poem

It was so strange,

We had not known each other long.

It did not matter.

If I were a singer you would be my song.

Afterthought

So you were Lindy.

One short summertime you gave to me.

Now you are gone

But still the sweetness lingers into time to be.

Did you guess, Lindy,

How little I had know of love before?

What did you feel,

After we had parted, to meet again no more?

But you were Lindy.

Neither you nor I will ever grieve.

That is not good.

For it was right that while still friends we took our leave.

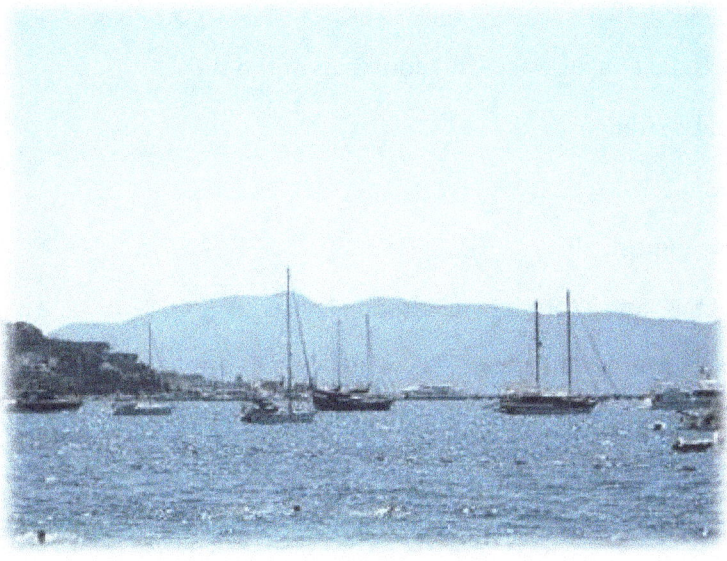

The Flowers of Dawn

A garland have I woven

Of the silver flowers of dawn.

All their putty I have by magic arts entwined

About the stems and leaves

Which I plucked from the misty transience of the dew

Today, before the sun awoke.

Your skin is soft, the softness

Of fresh peaches, newly ripe and still unbruised,

The colour of dark honey from the bees

That gather nectar from the silence of the hills.

And you are beautiful.

The flowers of dawn are sweet,

But wither quickly in the heat of day,

Their life is very short.

They bloom in silver sheen

Across the Lost Hills, just below the misty Mountains of the sky;

And here the world is strange.

They open as the sky takes fire

Just before sunrise comes.

Their tiny silver petals form a carpet far across the hills

Upon the dawning of Midsummer Day,

And wither as the first direct rays of the sun

Lance down upon them.

But I went out,

And, at the moment as prescribed in ancient lore,

I plucked the flowers of dawn,

And wove an everlasting garland of their beauty

In the misty dampness just before the dawn.

And this is yours,

A symbol of my love for you.

And all their everlasting purity is yours,

This has been granted by the Sower of the Seeds

When first he planted dawn flowers

In some far gone time.

A garland I have woven

Of the silver flowers of dawn,

Plucked from the everlasting morning dew.

Glory

So in the beauty of the painted morning skies

I see the hand of one who is the master artist,

At work upon a mighty canvas with the sun for brush before I rise,

With boldness and finesse no hand of mortal man can match,

Though all the human race attempts, no matter yet how hard it tries.

And the Sins of the Father........

Adam he stood in the garden,

Eve, his wife, by his side.

His maker called out to the first of men,

"Adam, son, why do you hide?"

Adam came out from the bushes,

Wearing a fig leaf he came,

"Lord, when you came we were naked,

The thought of it filled us with shame."

"Who told you that we were naked?"

The Lord asked his child in surprise.

"The serpent advised us to taste the fruit,

We ate, and we opened our eyes."

The brow of the Lord clouded over,

"You broke faith with your Father," He said.

"Go out from here to return nevermore."

So out from the garden man fled.

So through the ages the children

Of Adam, the father of men,

Have sought in vain for a method

To enter the Garden again.

So through the ages our children

Will ask us why nothing availed.

But we cannot teach them the way to truth,

We can only teach them how we failed.

Forgotten Time

The sun has gone,

His journey of the day across the heav'n

Is finished; daylight dies,

And, dying, leaves behind

The strange half-world of twilight,

A temporary station of the day,

Part sensed, and ill defined.

A time of unreality

When, thrown into confusion

By the air of unfamiliar half-time,

Experience and dream

Are fused within the mind

Into a shifting broken unity.

The air is liquid, sweet

As honey is, and warm;

A summer day has passed.

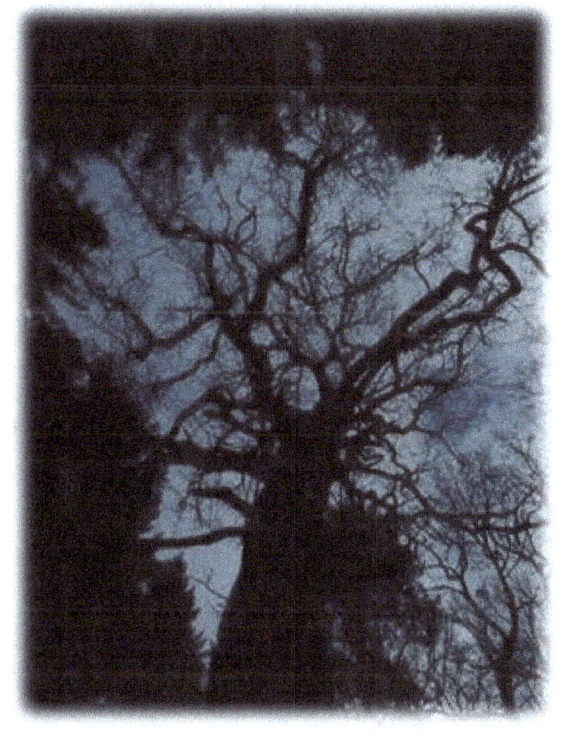

The western hills lie, crouched in silhouette,

So softly black and distant to the sky,

In which, above the last remaining wisps of pink,

The legacy of sunset,

Is set the jewel of Venus, star of evening.

The beauty and the silence of this world

Grow in the mystic atmosphere,

And senses, drunk with grandeur

From trying to appreciate the whole,

Fail in the viewing of the smallest part.

And then effect is shattered twilight dies

With the scream

Of some hunted creature of the day,

A victim of the night, For night has come.

Cain

You were the slayer, Cain.

You the destroyer of mankind.

You in your jealous hatred.

Oh, poor Cain,

Suff'ring the first inferiority complex.

I know how you feel.

Oh Cain, there was no need

To play your tragic act out to its close.

Your offering might have proved acceptable.

Instead you were destruction,

And the strong and upright elder son

Brought to the earth corruption for a second time.

See now, a wheat ear, growing from a socket of your brother's skull.

Oh do not pluck it Cain.

Go to your mother.

Tell her of the crime you have committed on her son.

Beg her forgiveness, Cain,

And wash the blood off in the tears the earth will cry.

And listen to me Cain.

I am your brother too,

I am your son.

For I am Cain

And I am lost in all eternity.

Bridge

The bridge gate has been locked and rusting many years,

The old boards rotting:

Some are lost, and holes gape.

Through them I can see the river

Many feet below.

The old bridge, derelict and useless,

Is a bridge no longer.

Many years its function has been
       taken

By a newer, stronger,

Twice as big, but only half as
       beautiful,

(Or twice as ugly. Much depends

On how one views the situation.)

Now the tendons of the old bridge

Rust away beneath the shady trees,

And no-one cares.

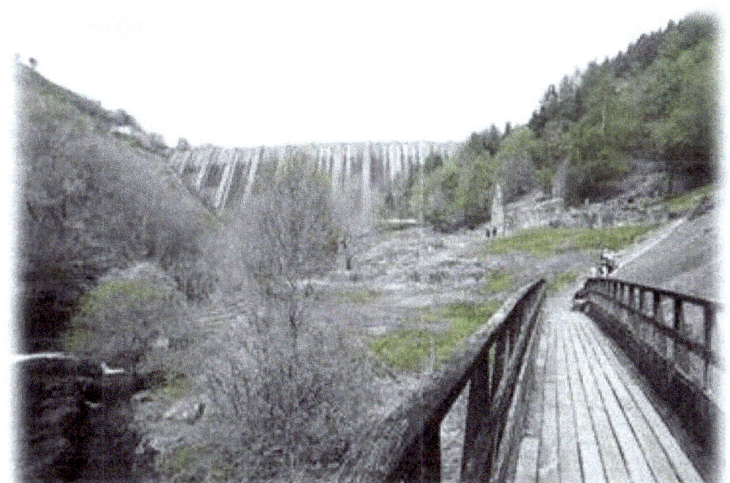

The only memories will be mine

To bridge the gap 'twixt when it was and is not there.

And one day the new bridge too will rot,

Decay away.

And what will happen then?

I do not know.

Nor have I any pressing reason that I care.

The bridge has served its purpose.

Let it die.

Lara

Searching,

I am always searching for my Lara,

My Bird of Fire,

My true love's inspiration.

For the one who, for my whole life,

Will provide me with the poetry I need.

So I wander restless,

Wander through crowds, alone,

Examining each face

For one which I will recognise.

Although I do not know what visage this will be,

Or fair or dark

Or any style of feature,

Yet I'll know her,

And in shared perception

She will know me too.

And in that moment

I will find the meaning of my life,

And all truth will be mine.

Icarus

"Icarus, my son, you should not fly so high,

For though those wings you use are made with eagle's plumes,

Plucked from the monarchs of the empty sky,

Yet I fear I will see my son in harm,

For they are only fixed with wax,

And in the cloudless sky the sun is very warm."

Oh no my aged father, you are wrong

To think mankind to such a problem yields.

For your son Icarus is man, and see,

I have supplied myself with radiation shields."

Pilgrimage

And thus will I

Make pilgrimage to Suilven

Far in the Northland.

Wastewild country, bare and old;

And old.

King above all

The planted desert of the hills,

The deep ancient watery wasteland there.

And thus,

By virtue of my pilgrimage,

Will prove myself

A man.

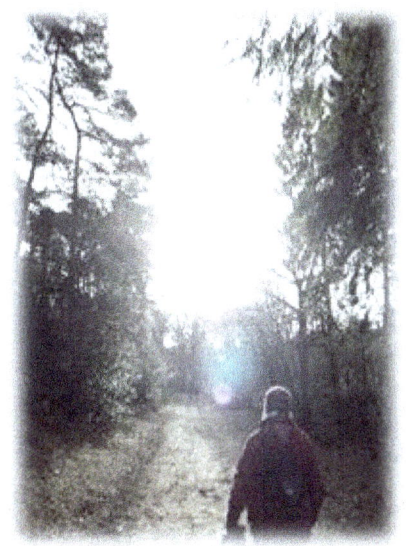

My Country

Return.

One day I will return,

I have no choice. But I know

I do not want the choice.

I will return to a wild and lonely land,

Where, amid the grandeur and the glory

Of the grey and purple hills,

My soul will find fulfilment,

And the torment

By which it is yet ravaged

Shall be stilled.

I will stand against the wind

On a bare mountain,

Looking across a raw hillside

As old as time, nay, older than time itself,

And watch as

The grey rain drifts across the sombre purple hillside,

And over the deep surface of the black loch.

Sweet grey drift.

I will watch, in the washed out whiteness

Of a spring sky,

A single solitary speck

Hang motionless, stiller than silence,

The buzzard, little king of the empty sky.

Across the green-stained, grey washed rocks

A shadow slips.

Look up!

There, nearly in the eye of the cold sun,

I see him,

A mighty warrior in a once mighty land.

Virile,

The overlord, the eagle, strides across the vastness

Of nothing.

There is nothing here.

Nothing!

Then why must I return to this
       land?

Yet I will return

Home.

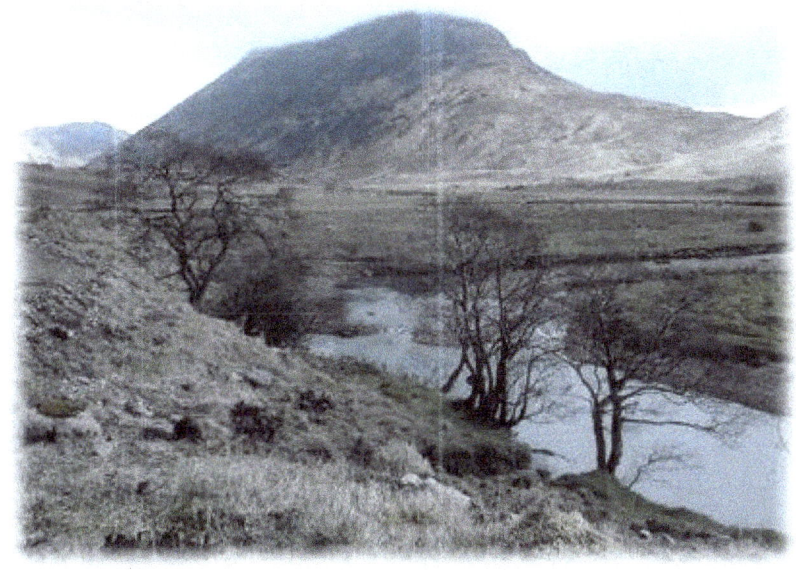

Toli

And then at Toli

Which was so incredibly beautiful

I felt somehow that I would stay forever,

I stood there, looking at the rain spoiled surface of the water,

Contemplating life

Beneath the red and yellow trees.

And then I walked into the village,

Spoke a little English,

Turned around,

And left.

Night

This is the hour.

A time of velvet depths,

The warmth, the silky softness

Of the dark,

The cobweb moonlight

Silvering its peace.

But also can the hour

Be that of growing tension, fear,

The backward glance that only is the sign

Of fast approaching terror.

When shadows move

And every zephyr breathes a devil's will.

When peace of both the mind and atmosphere

Is shattered by the agony of death

Of victims of the predators of night.

A time of mystery,

Which, suspenseful, comes

Along with swirling mist

And enigmatic, soft, sound deadened, moves.

Relentless comes, departs.

Which none can change.

The night.

Lost Love

My life has lost its sweetness

And the sun is cold.

The first sharp frost of Winter,

Coming early in the Spring,

Has taken all the newly flowering
                buds,

And desolation reigns.

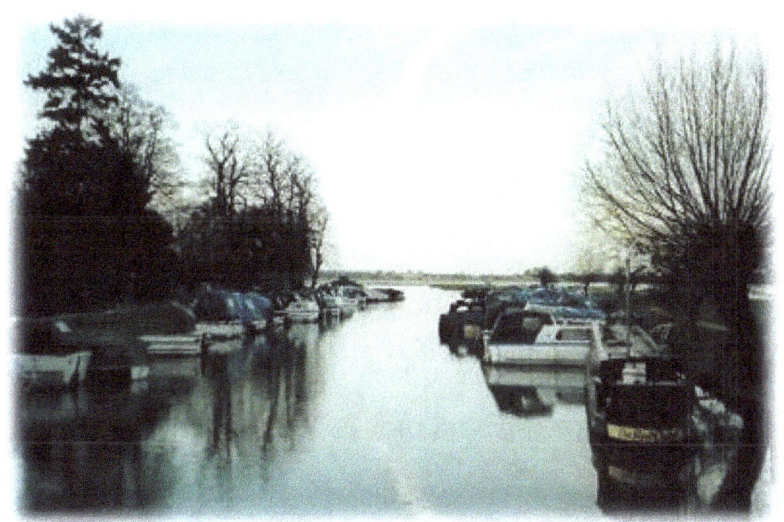

The bare trees cry in sorrow

For their childish. All the beauty

That I saw a little time ago

Is dead. The warmth you brought,

Which could have saved them, failed to last.

And so, too delicate to stand alone

Against the elements,

The fragile blossoms die.

What can I do?

The spring is over, but the summer has not come.

The clouds obscure the sun

Day after dreary day;

While I exist, no more,

And fill the void behind my mind

With soft and slow self-pitying songs

Of sadness.

The Paradise Seeker

The long dead days of youth and my simplicity,

Finished forever,

I am not a man of pride.

I have memories that no man can take from me,

Though there is much

That I would rather hide.

Where were you in the hour when most I needed you?

Vanished completely

As dreams melt with the dawn.

So nothing happens that I can define as new.

In melancholy

Is each new day born.

For I have not kept truth with he I could have been,

Lost absolutely,

Nobility and truth.

I made the dark to hide the things I should have seen.

Now it is over,

I have lost my youth.

The Staircase of the Night

The staircase of the night is lined with trees and ferns.

A gentle place.

The stairs are moss on stone.

The moon is shining softly through the trees,

Casting strange shadows on the gloom.

The stairs wind upwards,

Turn first this way, than that,

Sometimes wind arrow straight between the trees,

The slender silver birches

With still young covering shining silver,

Softly silver, in the moon.

And every now and then I start to climb.

I take this narrow path between the trees,

To find the poets land of gentle dreams,

Resting a little where some stream,

Some rivulet of silver,

Chasing and tumbling by the stair between the trees,

Which rise to left

And fall away to right;

And here I drink, refresh,

And start again

The weary climb up through the dark.

Until the sun shall rise,

Blistering and blasting with its daytime heat,

Destroying all around,

Drying the streams,

Moss to dust,

Trees to ash,

And I must find another

Staircase through the dark, to reach the poet's land of gentle dreams.

The Rains

The cold warm rains of January,

False end of winter,

Melt the snow to slush

And flood the streams.

February.

Winterain.

Cold from the sea.

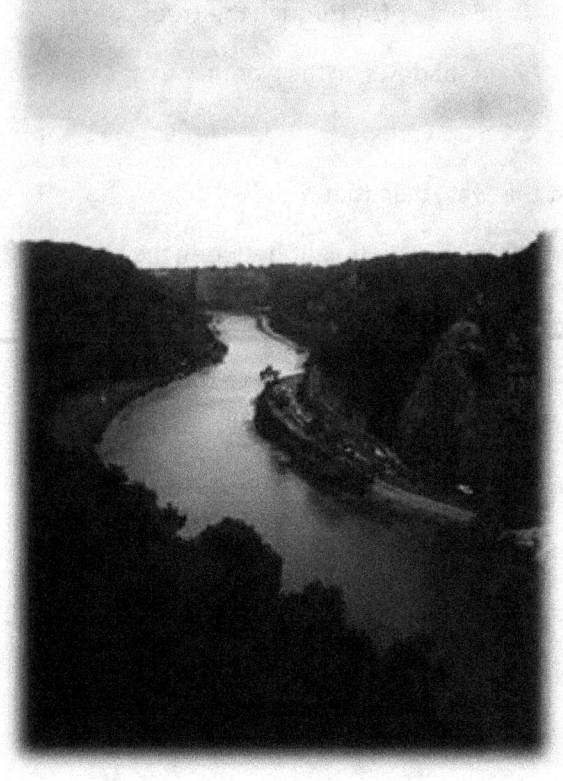

March,

Harbinger of spring,

The rain is hard

And clean and fresh.

Cleanses the Earth Mother

Ready for the spring.

April rain is soft and warm,

Comes with the sun from the rainbow's end,

Falls gently on the thirsty land,

A pattern of diamonds set in the sky's white clouds.

The rains of May,

Our yearly surprise, they follow April sun,

Frustrating our wishes and hopes of summertime.

June, the thin grey drizzle,

Coming from the sky,

Drives bat and field alike

To seek the indoor dampness

Of the milling bodies

Drinking unexpected pints

At the pavilion bar.

Rain in July,

Torrent and deluge,

Floods from the sky,

Expends its strength too quickly,

Cannot last,

And soon is banished by the blazing sun.

August. Thunderheads

Are mounting high.

The price we pay for lolling in the sun.

The rains may last a week,

Though usually less,

We hope.

September, and the showers

Again bring rainbows in the afternoon.

The warm and gentle rains

Of spring.

October follows on.

The rains get harder,

Greyer. Showers increase in regularity

As autumn marches on.

Thin November rain.

Wind driven drizzle.

Cold and sharp.

It penetrates and chills

All grey November long

We wish December rains could turn to snow,

That Christmas may be white.

Instead the veil

That beats against our window pane

As we eat, take our cheer

Around the fire,

Is the December rain.

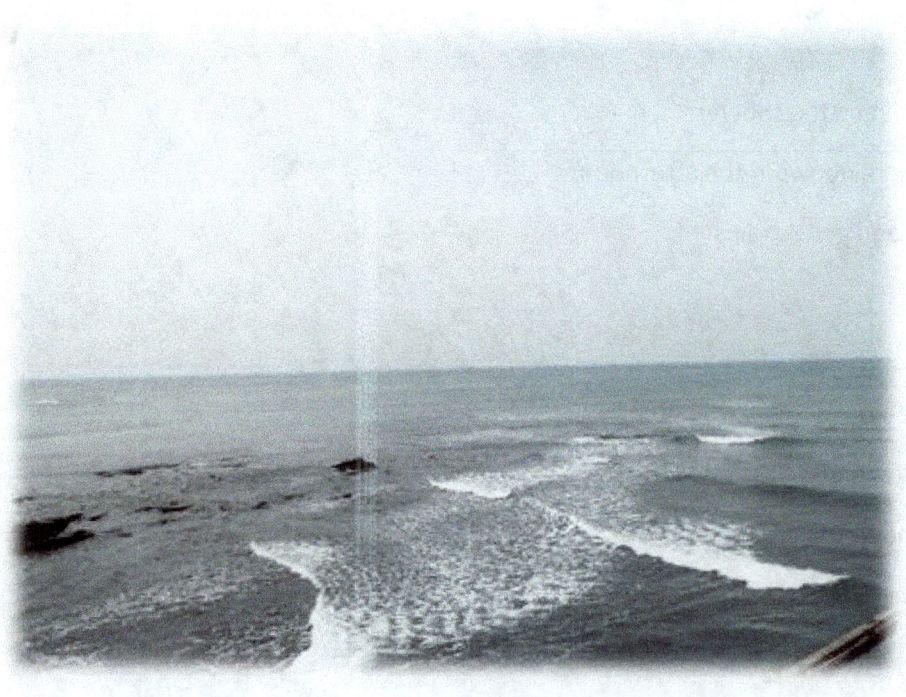

Philomel

Love, will you now return,

Singing the melody I yearn

To hear, composed for us alone to sing?

(I wrote the words, and you the tune,

A fragile harmony)

And shall we raise our voices soon.

Like birds the notes soar free

Flying up heavenwards on melodic wing,

Though now the tune is old,

The warm heart has grown cold,

And on the music duet is slowly settling.

Hark, though, for someone strikes the chords,

Can songs be sung again?

Our voices, dancing with the words,

Take up the old refrain.

Over the golden skies our song shall ring.

And from the deep sea of your eyes

My own song soars to dawning skies,

The new-old songster of the latest spring.

Oration

Something which might have been beautiful

Has withered, died.

There were no mourners at the funeral

And neither of them cried.

Time (six years) was bound to prove

Too much;

An obscene, slimy window,

Through which we saw,

But could do nothing more.

Our lips,

Our hearts, our fingertips

Came close, but could not touch.

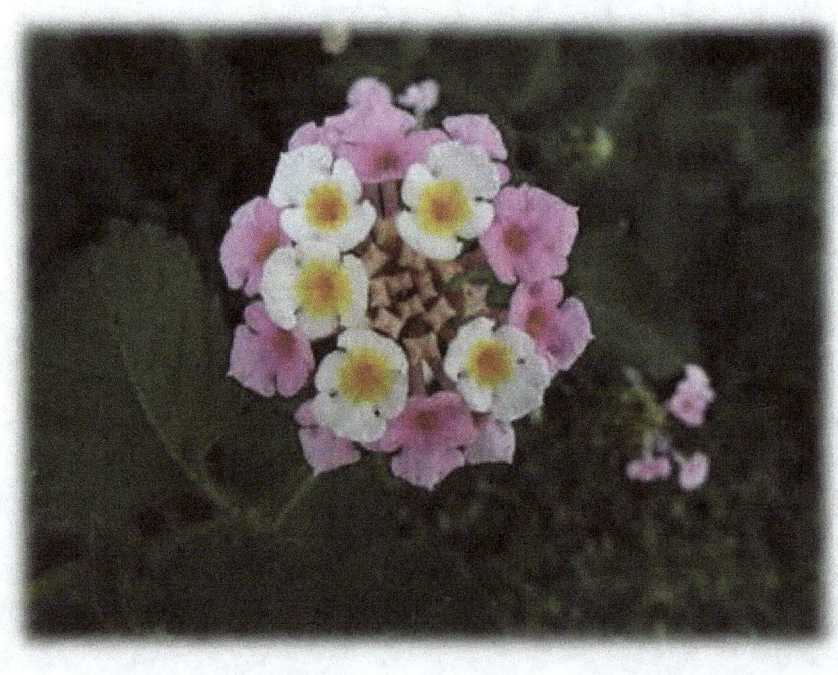

This for Marianne

Sunshine,

Sunshine, green trees

And a skylark singing,

Blue skies, peaceful earth

Surrounded by a hazy afternoon,

Corn and poppies blazing;

Or the coolness of the long grass

And the sweet refreshing shade of birches,

The soft light of a summer moon.

Soft rain, sunshine, rainbows,

And the shattering jewels of sunlight

On a peaceful sea.

Green grass, starlight,

Changing seasons,

The perfume of wild roses

And my love forever

In eternity.

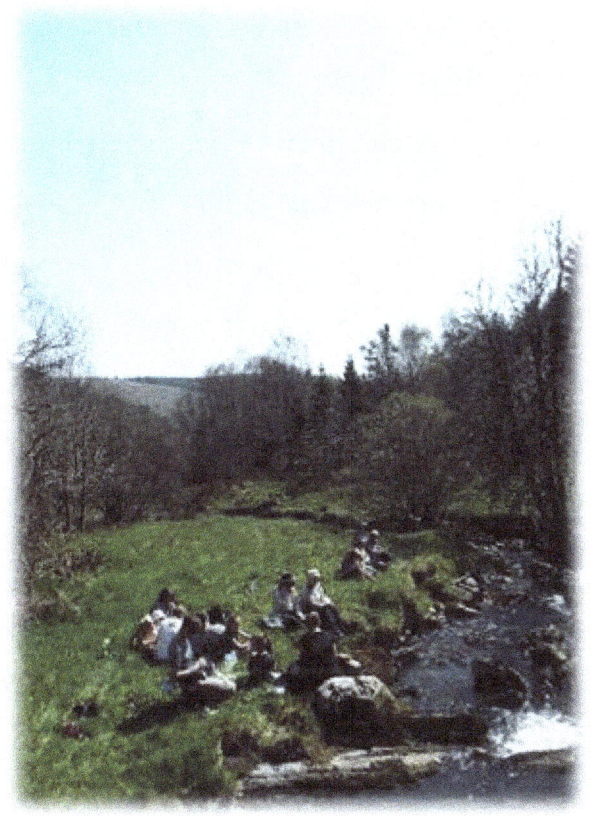

Aeroplane

Red trails in the sunset.

Fear

Over the golden valley of my dreams

I hover on wings,

But dare not light

For fear the green and verdant pastures seen from high

Are hiding deadly swamps,

And flowering trees have hives of serpents 'neath their leaves'.

Starlight Love

And in the peaceful warmth of future summer nights

My memory will turn to you.

And though its vision may be dimmed

By mists of passing, ever changing seasons,

Still you will be

More beautiful than shimmering, blazing starlight.

Or moon through trees, reflected off the stillness of the water.

A hazy memory, more insubstantial than a sunset breeze,

But floating in emotions dawn from all the universe above my head.

Yes, there is peace inherent in the atmosphere of such a night,

Peace, and a tender memory of you.

The tender, sweet-sad bitterness of memories of you.

Long Time Gone You Are, Lover

Once there was one,

A long time, long long time ago.

A rose, a vision.

A dream.

Perfection in an English flower in Maytime afternoon.

Once there was one,

A long time, long long time ago.

Hair of silken gold,

Fair skin

And blue eyes from the blue-eyed, clear-skied Northland.

Once there was one,

A long time, long long time ago.

She was a lonely one.

Her heart

Was in melancholy bound. I never found the key

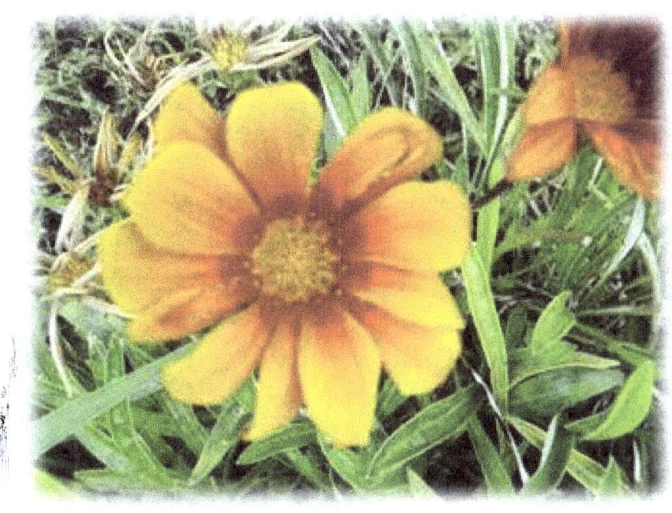

The Arena

Victim, I stand here

On the clean white sand

As yet unsullied by my blood.

The clean and level sand extends

Beyond the distant circular horizon

To the arena's walls;

And far away, as in a dream,

I hear the baying of the crowd

That craves my blood.

And lonely, at the centre of th' arena

I prepare to die.

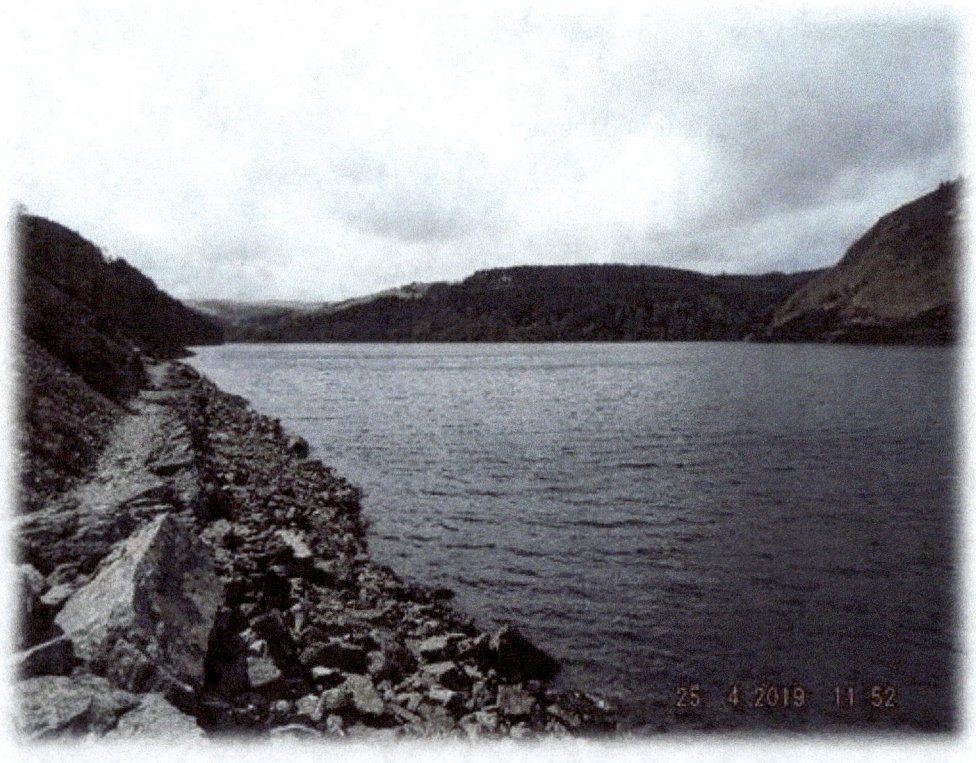

The Throw

Wait.

Wait, and concentrate;

Balancing, staring blankly far beyond horizons still unseen.

The movement starts,

And slowly, quickly,

Builds into a sinuous wave,

And gathering energies,

Rising, rising to perfection on the crest,

Explodes in action,

Climax,

In a thunderous roar of breaking power.

It is over, done.

The thrower looks again into the distance,

Turns,

And paces slowly back to let the next begin.

The Ungirt Runner

Sometimes, when I am running through the early morning,

(Spring, dew soaked grass and precious cobwebs,

Or the Sugar Ice of Winter crunching underneath my feet,

The cold air burning lungs and freezing fingers,

Running in cool and mist before the day,

(Stirring the blood, I pity

The fat and lazy slugs who're still abed)

Or when, through still warm air of early evening,

I speed along the lime tree'd avenues,

(Detached, remote, control my body

From a distance,)

Or running beneath the dappled shadows of the trees

To shelter from the searing heat of summer midday sun,

(Bounding down Shotover plain is good,

Until that last hill, rising through the beeches,)

Or when then night envelops me,

And I the hunter,

Run down the prey concealed in dark before me,

At times like these it is

(And not the races, not the cruelty,

The agony, the racking bodies, torture,

The destruction of the races)

I know the Glory and the Joy

That give me right to bear

The title of

The athlete.

The Bells

That was the first occasion that I crossed the line of hills

Dividing my own country from the lonely land far in the North,

The time I heard the true, clear ringing Bells of Dawn, the first and only time they rang,

To mark the new dawn of my life.

High on the hills above the barren land I stood

And heard the joyful ringing of the Golden Bells of Dawn.

The second time came later in my life, after the war between my people

And the nation of the North, (neither victorious)

Crossing the hills at sundown, in the copper heat before a storm,

I heard the bells ringing a song of Pain, carried away upon the First wild onslaught of the wind.

The third time was a very little later, and I crossed the hills at morning,

Travelling to claim for bride the one whom I had met the time before.

And as I reached the high point of the rocky mountain road

And looked down on the valley far below

The bells rang out in great unbridles Joy,

A shaft of sunlight striking through a cloud

To herald in a new and brighter day.

But the last time came, not as I crossed the hills to come,

But as I climbed the path into their lonely heart, alone,

The one great bell of iron tolled, a heavy note to match my leaden heart,

Losing the life that I had loved so well.

And always in my memory the echoes of the valley Bells ring true,

The wild Bells, ringing out the changing phases of my life.

But though the Bells were true in prophecy and mood

And wonderous purity of tone,

One question still remains unanswered, and seems like to be so for all time,

For there was never any bell tower in the far off Valley of the North.

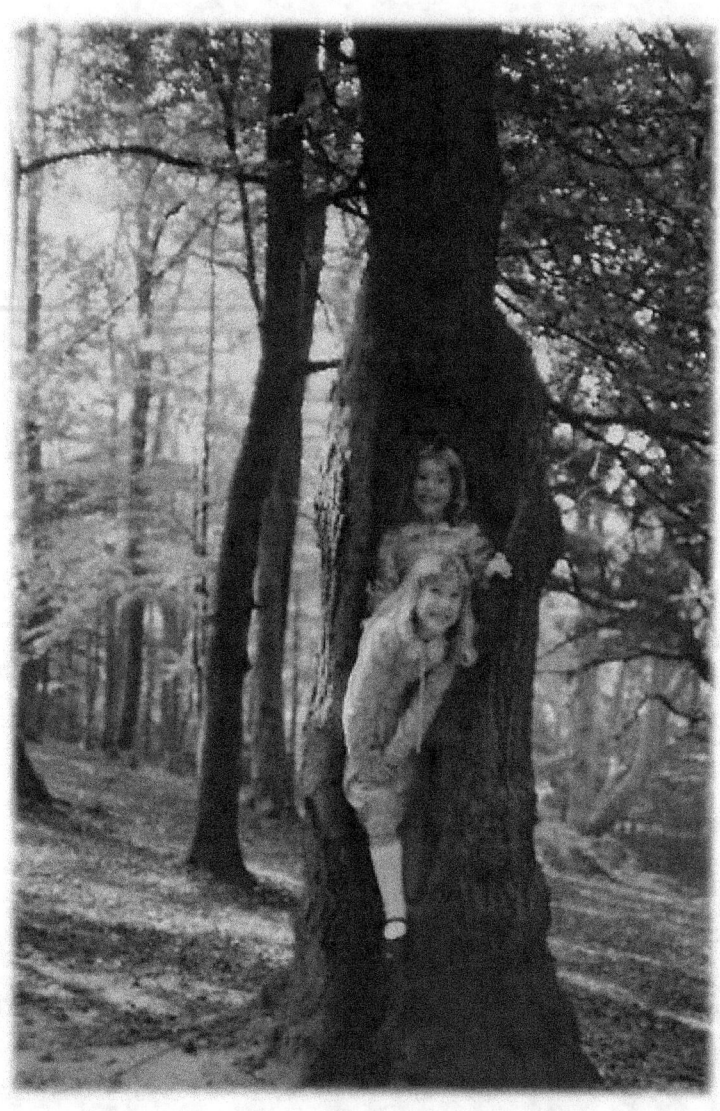

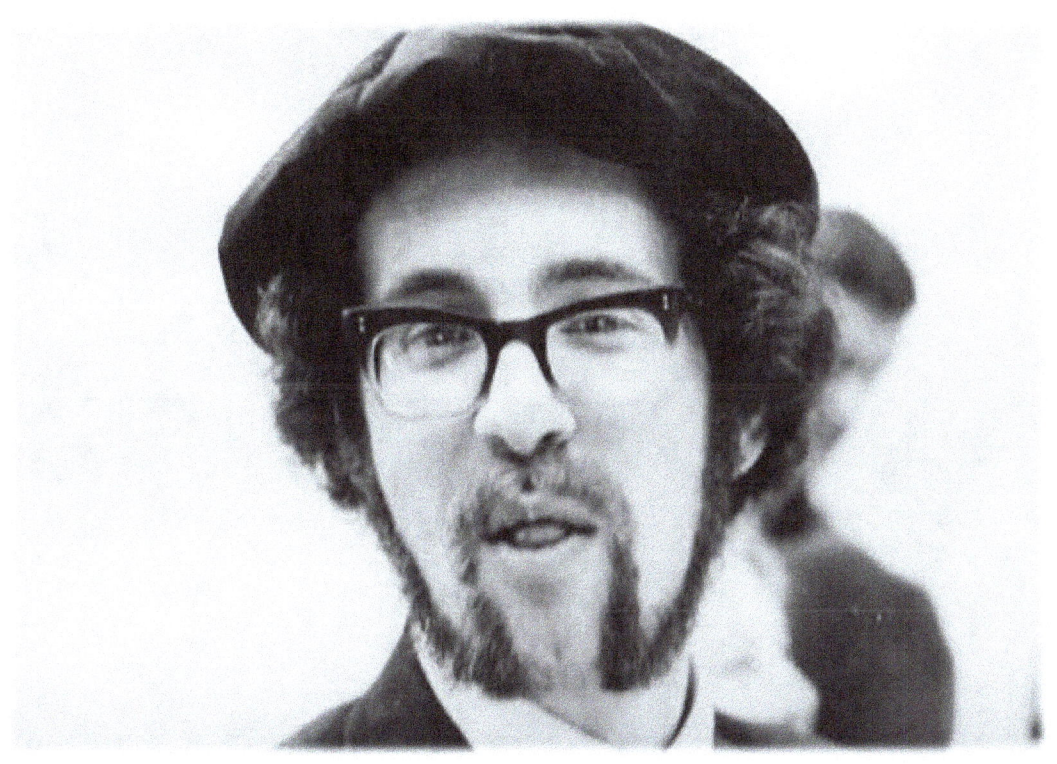

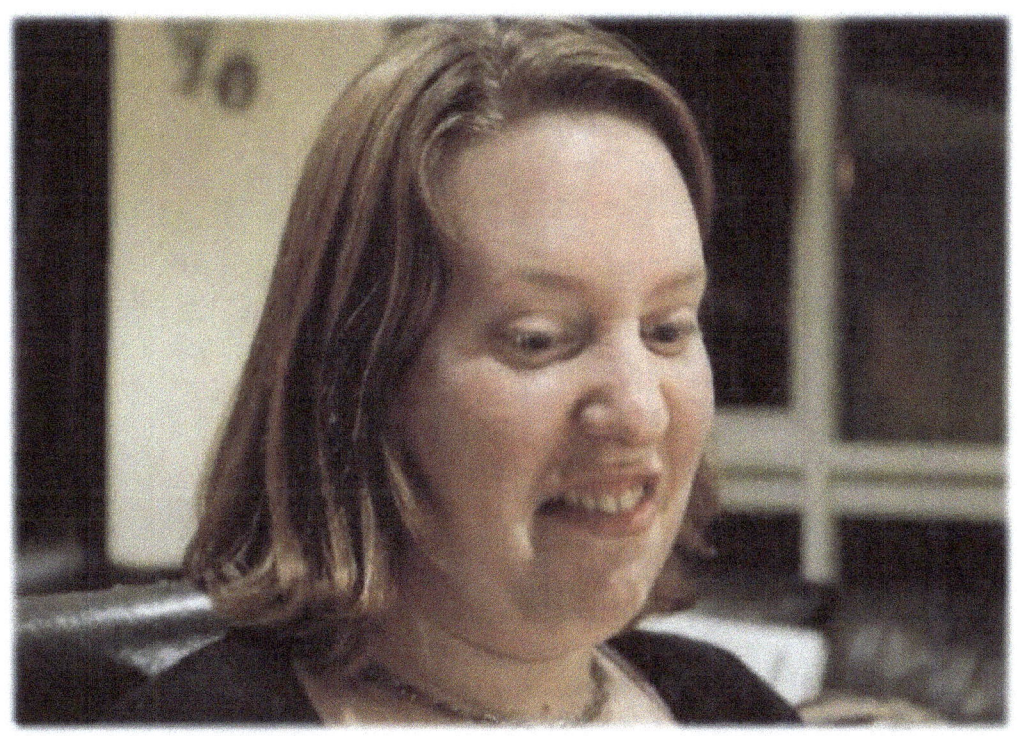

www.ingramcontent.com/pod-product-compliance
Lightning Source LLC
Chambersburg PA
CBHW081052170526
45158CB00007B/1946